U.S. HISTORY IN REVIEW

The Louisiana Purchase

By Kathryn Walton

Enslow Publishing

Please visit our website, www.enslow.com. For a free color catalog of all our high-quality books, call toll free 1-800-398-2504 or fax 1-877-980-4454.

Library of Congress Cataloging-in-Publication Data
Names: Walton, Kathryn, author.
Title: The Louisiana Purchase / Kathryn Walton.
Description: Buffalo, New York : Enslow Publishing, [2024] | Series: U.S. history in review | Includes index.
Identifiers: LCCN 2023009723 (print) | LCCN 2023009724 (ebook) | ISBN 9781978536210 (library binding) | ISBN 9781978536203 (paperback) | ISBN 9781978536227 (ebook)
Subjects: LCSH: Louisiana Purchase–Juvenile literature.
Classification: LCC E333 .W35 2024 (print) | LCC E333 (ebook) | DDC 973.4/6–dc23/eng/20230307
LC record available at https://lccn.loc.gov/2023009723
LC ebook record available at https://lccn.loc.gov/2023009724

Published in 2024 by
Enslow Publishing
2544 Clinton Street
Buffalo, NY 14224

Portions of this work were originally authored by Seth Lynch and published as *The Louisiana Purchase.* All new material in this edition authored by Kathryn Walton.

Designer: Leslie Taylor
Editor: Natalie Humphrey

Photo credits: Cover Jim Pruitt/Shutterstock.com; series art (grunge flag) Andrey Kuzmin/Shutterstock.com; series art (stamp icon) Stocker_team/Shutterstock.com; series art (font) santstock/Shutterstock.com; p. 5 Jose Gil /Shutterstock.com; p. 7 Roi de France/https://commons.wikimedia.org/wiki/File:TRAITÉ_DE_PARIS_10_FÉVRIER_1763_(France%2BGB%2BEspagne).jpg; p. 9 Everett Collection/Shutterstock.com; p. 11 Everett Collection/Shutterstock.com; p. 13 https://www.whitehousehistory.org/galleries/presidential-portraits/ https://commons.wikimedia.org/wiki/File:Official_Presidential_portrait_of_Thomas_Jefferson_(by_Rembrandt_Peale,_1800)(cropped).jpg; p. 15 Everett Collection/Shutterstock.com; p. 16 The U.S. National Archives/https://commons.wikimedia.org/wiki/File:Louisiana_Purchase_Treaty,_Page_1_(5553723360).jpg; p. 17 USCapitol/https://commons.wikimedia.org/wiki/File:Flickr_-_USCapitol_-_Louisiana_Purchase,_1803.jpg; p. 19 lazyllama/Shutterstock.com; p. 21 Dan Thornberg/Shutterstock.com; p. 23 Everett Collection/Shutterstock.com; p. 25 Dsdugan/https://commons.wikimedia.org/wiki/File:22-16-154-sacagawea.jpg; p. 27 Teresa Otto/Shutterstock.com; p. 28 Dimitrios Karamitros/Shutterstock.com; p. 29 Creative Jen Designs/Shutterstock.com.

Printed in the United States of America

CPSIA compliance information: Batch #CSENS24: For further information, contact Enslow Publishing at 1-800-398-2504.

Contents

Words in the glossary appear in ***bold*** *the first time they are used in the text.*

Claiming North America

Great Britain, Spain, and France each controlled large parts of North America at the beginning of the 1800s. France controlled a very large part right in the middle of North America. This was called Louisiana. It included an important shipping **port** called New Orleans.

Learn More

Louisiana was named after King Louis XIV. Louis XIV was the king of France when the country claimed Louisiana in 1682.

France Loses Louisiana

In 1762, France **ceded** part of Louisiana to Spain. The **Seven Years' War** was nearing its end. A few months later, in 1763, the **Treaty** of Paris ended the war. This treaty turned over other French land in North America to Great Britain.

Learn More

With Louisiana, Spain also controlled the Mississippi River and New Orleans.

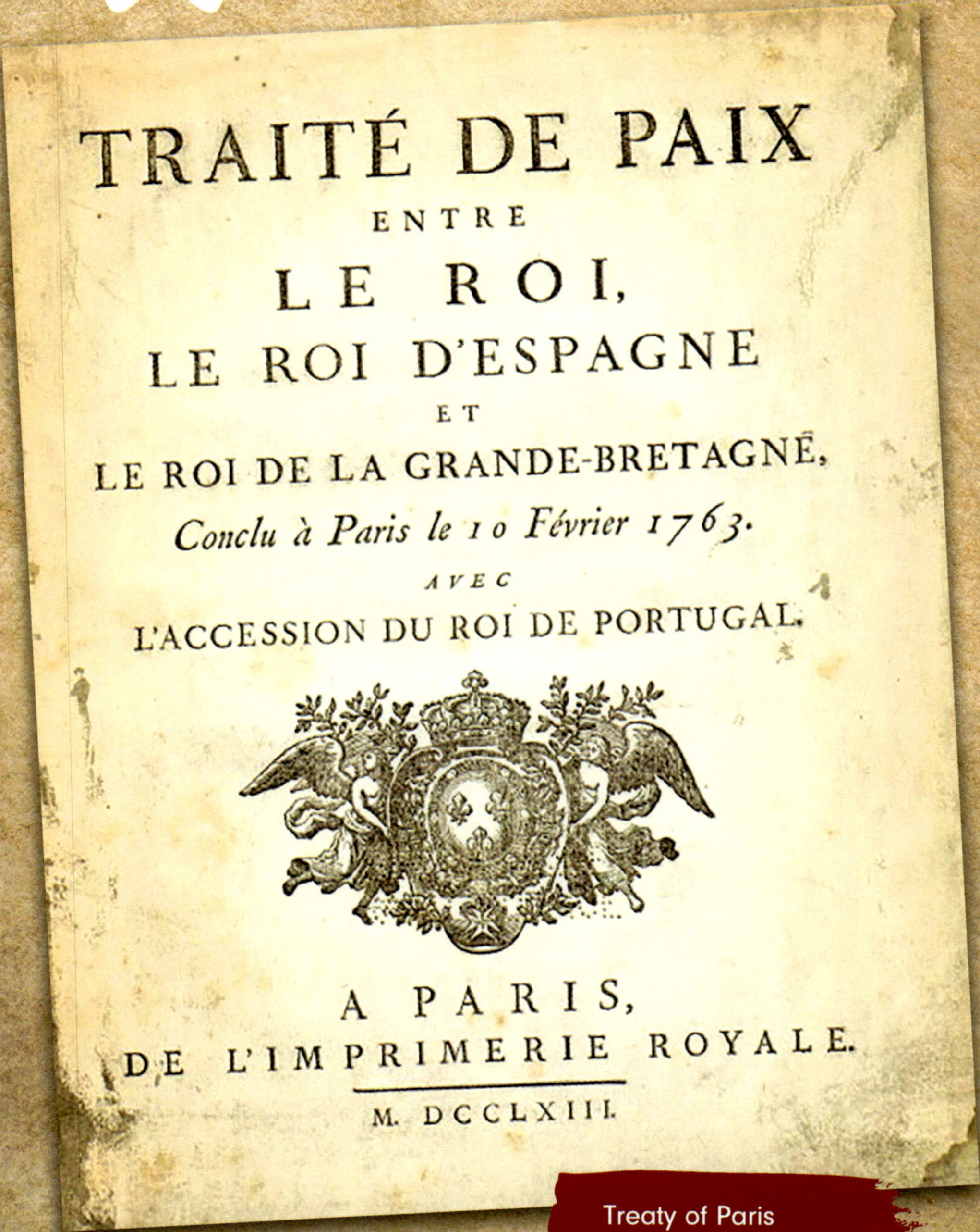

TRAITÉ DE PAIX

ENTRE

LE ROI,

LE ROI D'ESPAGNE

ET

LE ROI DE LA GRANDE-BRETAGNE,

Conclu à Paris le 10 Février 1763.

AVEC

L'ACCESSION DU ROI DE PORTUGAL.

A PARIS,

DE L'IMPRIMERIE ROYALE.

M. DCCLXIII.

Treaty of Paris

The French Revolution

In 1792, the French people **overthrew** their king. This was part of the French **Revolution**. A new leader named Napoleon Bonaparte later rose to power in the new government in 1799. Napoleon wanted to bring France back to into world power.

Learn More

Napoleon started out as a member of a French government called the Consulate. In 1804, though, he declared, or named, himself France's emperor, or ruler.

the French Revolution, 1789

Napoleon **convinced** the Spanish king to sign the Treaty of San Ildefonso. It gave the Louisiana **territory** back to France. The U.S. government began to worry that farmers would lose use of the Mississippi River and Port New Orleans. Spain had allowed the United States to use the river.

Learn More

The Mississippi River was the western border of the United States after the American Revolution. This was the war in which the United States became free of British control.

Napoleon Bonaparte

The United States Makes a Deal

President Thomas Jefferson wanted to stop the French from gaining more power in North America. In early 1802, Jefferson told the U.S. **minister** in Paris, France, to try to convince France not to take back Louisiana. If he couldn't, the minister was to offer to buy New Orleans.

Thomas Jefferson

Learn More

Robert R. Livingston was the U.S. minster to France. He told people in France that the United States was going to make an agreement with Great Britain. He knew Napoleon wouldn't want that to happen.

To help make a deal, Jefferson also sent James Monroe to France. The ministers were told they could spend $10 million on a land deal with France. But, as the ministers **negotiated** with the French, France offered them a $15 million deal for all of Louisiana.

James Monroe

Learn More

Monroe and Livingston weren't given the power to buy all of Louisiana. But it was such a good deal they did it anyway.

The Louisiana Purchase Treaty was agreed to in late April 1803. Mail from Europe took a long time to reach the United States back then. President Jefferson didn't find out about the agreement until July!

the Louisisana Purchase Treaty

LOUISIANA PURCHASE, 1803

Learn More

While he was happy with the deal, Jefferson worried the Senate wouldn't approve, or OK, it. Jefferson also worried the president didn't have the power to purchase, or buy, such a large piece of land.

In October 1803, the U.S. Senate voted and agreed the treaty should stand. This added around 828,000 square miles (2,144,510 sq km) of land to the United States. The Louisiana Territory was larger than Great Britain, France, Germany, Italy, Spain, and Portugal put together.

Learn More

Napoleon sold Louisiana because France didn't have enough forces to defend it, or keep it safe. The French also needed money in case a war with Great Britain began.

U.S. Capitol building, where the Senate votes

Unclear Borders

Not all the **boundaries** of the Louisiana Purchase were clear. The Mississippi River was the eastern boundary, and the Rocky Mountains were the western boundary. It took the United States, Great Britain, and Spain around 10 years to work out the other borders.

Mississippi River

Learn More

Great Britain and the United States agreed on the northern border in 1818. Spain agreed to the border in the southwest as well as modern-day Texas and Florida in 1819.

The Corps of Discovery

President Jefferson asked Captain Meriwether Lewis to explore the new Louisiana Territory. Lewis was joined by William Clark and about 30 other men. Together, they were called the Corps of Discovery. On May 14, 1804, the group set off on the Missouri River.

Lewis and Clark and their exploration group, the Corps of Discovery

Learn More

The Corps of Discovery was looking for a water route, or path, to the Pacific Ocean. They thought the Missouri River might be part of that route.

During their journey, or trip, the Corps of Discovery added two **interpreters** to their group. They would meet as many as 50 different Native American groups on their journey, and the interpreters helped them talk with these groups. One interpreter was a French Canadian fur trader. The other was his wife, Sacagawea.

Learn More

Sacagawea was a Shoshone woman. She brought her baby son along with her on the journey. She knew people in some of the Native groups they met along the way.

The White House Museum

Lewis and Clark sent many artifacts, or things made by humans in the past, to Jefferson during their journey. To display, or show off, these artifacts, Jefferson turned the front hall of the White House into a museum. A museum is a building in which things of interest are displayed.

This display in a Lewis and Clark museum contains artifacts like those given to Thomas Jefferson.

Learn More

At the White House Museum, the public could see what the American West was like. It had many things, including animal skins and Native American art. It also had two grizzly bear cubs living in a pen outside.

Mapping Louisiana

In 1805, the Corps of Discovery reached the Pacific Ocean. They mapped the new land in the United States as they traveled. They learned more about the plants, animals, and Native peoples living there. Their work would help people for years to come.

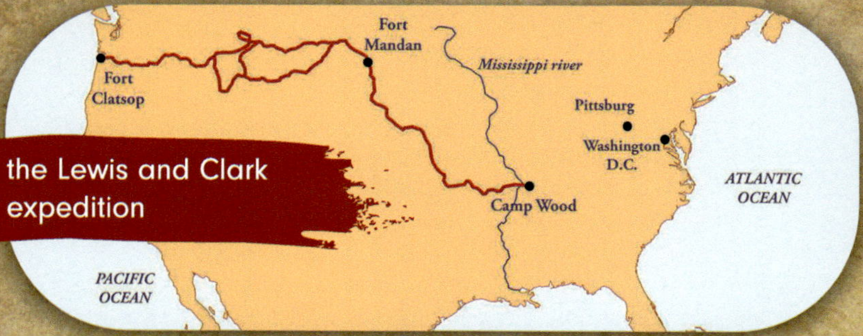

the Lewis and Clark expedition

Learn More

The Louisiana Purchase was later divided into the states of Arkansas, Louisiana, Missouri, Nebraska, Iowa, North Dakota, and South Dakota. It also became parts of Kansas, Minnesota, Wyoming, Montana, and Colorado.

Timeline

1762
The Louisiana Territory is ceded to Spain.

1795
Spain gives the United States the right to use the Mississippi River to ship American goods through New Orleans.

1800
France and Spain sign the Treaty of San Ildefonso, which gave the Louisiana Territory back to France.

1803
The United States sends James Monroe to France to help negotiate a land purchase from France.

April 1803
The Louisiana Purchase Treaty is agreed to by the United States and France.

October 1803
The Louisiana Purchase Treaty is approved by the Senate.

May 1804
The Corps of Discovery sets out on the Missouri River.

Glossary

boundary: Something that marks the limit of an area or place.

cede: To give control of something to someone else.

convince: To make a person agree to something.

interpreter: Someone who can tell and share the meaning of another language.

minister: A person who goes to a foreign land on behalf of their country.

negotiate: To try to come to an agreement.

overthrow: To force a leader or government out of power.

port: A city or town where ships can load and unload goods.

revolution: A movement to overthrow an established government.

Seven Years' War: A war that lasted from 1756 to 1763 and included many powerful countries in Europe. This war included struggles between Great Britain and France about control of North America.

territory: An area of land that a group or person considers to be their own and will fight to defend.

treaty: An agreement between countries.

For More Information

Books

Krensky, Stephen. *Meriwether Lewis and William Clark*. New York, NY: Crabtree Publishing, 2023.

Shea, Therese. *The Louisiana Purchase and the Lewis and Clark Expedition*. New York, NY: Britannica Educational Publishing, 2018.

Website

National Geographic Kids
kids.nationalgeographic.com/history/article/lewis-and-clark
Learn more about the journey of Lewis and Clark.

Publisher's note to educators and parents: *Our editors have carefully reviewed this website to ensure that it is suitable for students. Many websites change frequently, however, and we cannot guarantee that a site's future contents will continue to meet our high standards of quality and educational value. Be advised that students should be closely supervised whenever they access the internet.*

Index